• THIS JOURNAL BELONGS TO •

....

....

....

• DATE •

....

Her children arise up, and call her blessed.

PROVERBS 31:28 KJV

A mother has the special gift of always speaking true.

A mother gets the praise or blame if skies be dark or blue.

A mother is a doctor, a joiner or a vet,

the jobs a mother cannot do have not been heard of yet.

A mother is a power all wise, a tyrant or a saint,

an oracle, a paragon, with smart ideas or quaint.

Whatever else she may be, a mother knows full well,

a house could never be a home without her charming spell.

A child's hand in yours—what tenderness and power it arouses.

You are instantly the very touchstone of wisdom and strength.

MARJORIE HOLMES

What is home? A roof to keep out the rain? Four walls
to keep out the wind? Floors to keep out the cold?
Yes, but home is more than that. It is the laugh of a baby,
the song of a mother, the strength of a father, warmth
of loving hearts, lights from happy eyes, kindness, loyalty,
comradeship. Home is first school and first church for young
ones, where they learn what is right, what is good,
and what is kind, where they go for comfort when they are
hurt or sick; where joy is shared and sorrow eased;
where fathers and mothers are respected and loved,
where children are wanted; where the simplest food is good
enough for kings because it is earned; where money is not
as important as loving-kindness; where even the tea kettle
sings from happiness. That is home. God bless it!

The godly walk with integrity;
blessed are their children after them.

PROVERBS 20:7 NLT

Most of all the other beautiful things in life come by twos and threes, by dozens and hundreds. Plenty of roses, stars, sunsets, rainbows, brothers and sisters, aunts and cousins, comrades and friends—but only one mother in the whole world.

KATE DOUGLAS WIGGIN

A mother is...one who can take the place of all others, but whose place no one else can take.

G. MERMILLOD

The Lord bless thee, and keep thee: the LORD make his face shine upon thee, and be gracious unto thee: the LORD lift up his countenance upon thee, and give thee peace.

NUMBERS 6:24–26 KJV

A mother is not a person; she's a miracle.

MARY HOLLINGSWORTH

The loveliest masterpiece of the heart of God

is the heart of a mother.

THÉRÈSE OF LISIEUX

Oh, that their hearts would be inclined to fear me

and keep all my commands always, so that it might

go well with them and their children forever!

DEUTERONOMY 5:29 NIV

Watch what God does, and then you do it, like children who learn proper behavior from their parents. Mostly what God does is love you. Keep company with him and learn a life of love. Observe how Christ loved us. His love was not cautious but extravagant. He didn't love in order to get something from us but to give everything of himself to us. Love like that.

EPHESIANS 5:1–2 MSG

Open your hearts to the love God instills....
God loves you tenderly. What He gives you
is not to be kept under lock and key, but to be shared.

MOTHER TERESA

I pray that your love will overflow more and more,
and that you will keep on growing in knowledge and understanding.

PHILIPPIANS 1:9 NLT

Let God have you, and let God love you—
and don't be surprised if your heart begins
to hear music you've never heard
and your feet learn to dance as never before.

MAX LUCADO

O the pure delight of a single hour
that before Thy throne I spend,
When I kneel in prayer, and with Thee, my God,
I commune as friend with friend!

FANNY J. CROSBY

Let the godly rejoice.
Let them be glad in God's presence.
Let them be filled with joy.

PSALM 68:3 NLT

Remember the things I have done in the past.

For I alone am God!

I am God, and there is none like me.

Only I can tell you the future

before it even happens.

Everything I plan will come to pass,

for I do whatever I wish.

ISAIAH 46:9–10 NLT

Every person's life is a fairy tale written by God's fingers.

HANS CHRISTIAN ANDERSEN

For I know the plans I have for you," declares the LORD,

"plans to prosper you and not to harm you,

plans to give you hope and a future."

JEREMIAH 29:11 NIV

They might not need me;

but they might.

I'll let my head be just in sight;

A smile as small as mine might be

Precisely their necessity.

EMILY DICKINSON

Jesus said, "Let the children come to me.

Don't stop them! For the Kingdom of Heaven

belongs to those who are like these children."

MATTHEW 19:14 NLT

Instant availability without continuous presence

is probably the best role a mother can play.

L . BAILYN

Your love, LORD, reaches to the heavens,

your faithfulness to the skies.

Your righteousness is like the highest mountains,

your justice like the great deep.

You, LORD, preserve both people and animals.

How priceless is your unfailing love, O God!

People take refuge in the shadow of your wings.

They feast on the abundance of your house;

you give them drink from your river of delights.

For with you is the fountain of life;

in your light we see light.

PSALM 36:5–9 NIV

God's love is like a river springing up in the Divine Substance

and flowing endlessly

through His creation, filling all things with life

and goodness and strength.

THOMAS MERTON

If you then...know how to give good gifts to your children,
how much more will your Father who is in heaven
give good things to those who ask him!

MATTHEW 7:11 ESV

Maybe all I could do was mother.... And yet, why did I feel
so fulfilled when I bedded down three kids between clean
sheets? What if raising and instilling values in three children
and turning them into worthwhile human beings would be
the most important contribution I ever made in my lifetime?

ERMA BOMBECK

In the effort to give good and comforting answers
to the young questioners whom we love, we very often
arrive at good and comforting answers for ourselves.

RUTH GOODE

Faces pressed at a window pane

Watching for someone to come again.

And I am the someone they want to see—

These are the joys life gives to me.

So let me come home at night and rest

With those who know I have done my best;

Let my [loved ones] rejoice and my children smile,

And know by their love that I'm worth while.

For this is conquest and world success—

A home where abideth happiness.

EDGAR A. GUEST

Home is where there's one to love;

Home is where there's one to love us!

ROY LESSIN

He settles the childless woman in her home

as a happy mother of children. Praise the LORD.

PSALM 113:9 NIV

The sunshine dancing on the water, the lulling sound
of waves rolling into the shore, the glittering stars
against the night sky—all God's light, His warmth,
His majesty—our Father of light reaching out to us,
drawing each of us closer to Himself.

WENDY MOORE

By putting the gift of yearning for God into every human
being's heart, God at the same time draws all people made
in God's image to God's self and into their own true selves.

ROBERTA BONDI

Draw near to God and He will draw near to you.

JAMES 4:8 NKJV

For my dear little child I'd lasso the moon

and give you my love on a silver spoon.

I'd run 'round the world and back again, too,

to grant you the hope of days bright and new.

But all that I have and all that I do

is nothing compared to God's love for you.

Everyone was meant to share

God's all-abiding love and care;

He saw that we would need to know

a way to let these feelings show....

So God made hugs.

JILL WOLF

Be devoted to one another in love.

Honor one another above yourselves.

ROMANS 12:10 NIV

You have made known to me the paths of life;

you will fill me with joy in your presence.

ACTS 2:28 NIV

The best things are nearest...light in your eyes,

flowers at your feet,

duties at your hand, the path of God just before you.

ROBERT LOUIS STEVENSON

Thy word is a lamp unto my feet,

and a light unto my path.

PSALM 119:105 KJV

The God who created, names, and numbers the stars
in the heavens also numbers the hairs of my head....
He pays attention to very big things and to very small ones.
What matters to me matters to Him, and that changes my life.

ELISABETH ELLIOT

What matters supremely is not the fact that I know God,
but the larger fact which underlies it—the fact that He knows me.
I am graven on the palms of His hands. I am never out of His mind.
All my knowledge of Him depends on His sustained initiative
in knowing me. I know Him because He first knew me,
and continues to know me.

J. I. PACKER

Every good gift and every perfect gift is from above,
and cometh down from the Father of lights,
with whom is no variableness, neither shadow of turning.

JAMES 1:17 KJV

There is nothing higher and stronger and more wholesome and useful for life in later years than some good memory, especially a memory connected with childhood, with home. Those who carry many such memories with them into life are safe to the end of their days.

FYODOR DOSTOEVSKY

Favorite people, favorite places,
favorite memories of the past...
These are the joys of a lifetime...
these are the things that last.

Only the living can praise you as I do today.
Each generation tells of your faithfulness to the next.

ISAIAH 38:19 NLT

A family is a "gallery of memories" to those who have been blessed by the presence of children.

DR. JAMES DOBSON

Satisfy us in the morning with your unfailing love,

that we may sing for joy and be glad all our days.

Make us glad for as many days as you have afflicted us,

for as many years as we have seen trouble.

May your deeds be shown to your servants,

your splendor to their children.

May the favor of the Lord our God rest on us;

establish the work of our hands for us—

yes, establish the work of our hands.

PSALM 90:14–17 NIV

Today Jesus is working just as wonderful works

as when He created the heaven and the earth.

His wondrous grace, His wonderful omnipotence,

is for His child who trusts Him, even today.

CHARLES E. HURLBURT AND T. C. HORTON

Little drops of water,

Little grains of sand,

Make the mighty ocean

And the pleasant land.

Little deeds of kindness,

Little words of love,

Help to make earth happy

Like the heaven above.

JULIA FLETCHER CARNEY

As we grow in our capacities to see and enjoy the joys
that God has placed in our lives, life becomes a glorious
experience of discovering His endless wonders.

I will show wonders in the heavens and on the earth.

JOEL 2:30 NIV

A child's spirit is like a child: you can never

catch it by running after it;

you must stand still, and for love, it will soon itself come back.

ARTHUR MILLER

You are the gate through which it came into the world,

and you will be allowed to have charge of it for a period;

after that it will leave you and blossom out into its own free life—

and there it is, for you to watch, living its life in freedom.

AGATHA CHRISTIE

Use your freedom to serve one another in love;

that's how freedom grows.

GALATIANS 5:13 MSG

Mother is the name for God

in the lips and hearts of little children.

WILLIAM MAKEPEACE THACKERAY

There are two lasting bequests we can give our children.

One of these is roots; the other, wings.

HODDING CARTER

Like an eagle that rouses her chicks

and hovers over her young,

so he spread his wings to take them up

and carried them safely on his pinions.

DEUTERONOMY 32:11 NLT

A mother's love gives us wings.

If one is joyful, it means that one is faithfully living for God, and that nothing else counts; and if one gives joy to others one is doing God's work. With joy without and joy within, all is well.

JANET ERSKINE STUART

Our hearts were made for joy. Our hearts were made to enjoy the One who created them. Too deeply planted to be much affected by the ups and downs of life, this joy is a knowing and a being known by our Creator. He sets our hearts alight with radiant joy.

The joy of the LORD is your strength.

NEHEMIAH 8:10 KJV

A garden of God is our childhood, each day
A festival radiant with laughter and play.
M. J. LEBENSOHN

As the gardener is responsible for the produce
of their garden,
so the family is responsible for the character
and conduct of its children.

You shall be like a watered garden,
like a spring of water,
whose waters do not fail.
ISAIAH 58:11 ESV

If I had a single flower for every time I think about you,
I could walk forever in my garden.
CLAUDIA A. GRANDÍ

It is not how much we have,

but how much we enjoy, that makes happiness.

CHARLES H. SPURGEON

I will bless the LORD at all times:

his praise shall continually be in my mouth.

PSALM 34:1 KJV

Sometimes our thoughts turn back toward a corner in a forest,

or the end of a bank, or an orchard powdered with flowers,

seen but a single time…yet remaining in our hearts and leaving

in soul and body an unappeased desire which is not to be forgotten,

a feeling we have just rubbed elbows with happiness.

GUY DE MAUPASSANT

Our inner happiness depends not on what we experience but on

the degree of our gratitude to God, whatever the experience.

ALBERT SCHWEITZER

When she reviewed her parenting, she never thought...
of the good school, the advantages, as they were called.
No, what she felt she had given them was her attention:

her love, her caring, her willingness to listen.

MARGE PIERCY

What will your children remember?
Moments spent listening, talking, playing, and sharing

together may be the most important times of all.

GLORIA GAITHER

Come, my children, and listen to me,

and I will teach you to fear the LORD.

PSALM 34:11 NLT

The gift of listening is one of the best gifts you can give

your child, any time of the year.

You are valuable just because you exist. Not because of what you do or what you have done, but simply because you are. Just think about the way Jesus honors you...and smile.

MAX LUCADO

We are of such value to God that He came to live among us... and to guide us home. He will go to any length to seek us.... We can only respond by loving God for His love.

CATHERINE OF SIENA

We love him, because he first loved us.

1 JOHN 4:19 KJV

He paints the lily of the field,

Perfumes each lily bell;

If He so loves the little flowers,

I know He loves me well.

MARIA STRAUS

Look at the lilies of the field and how they grow.

They don't work or make their clothing, yet Solomon

in all his glory was not dressed as beautifully as they are.

MATTHEW 6:28–29 NLT

God cares for the world He created, from the rising of a nation

to the falling of the sparrow. Everything in the world lies

under the watchful gaze of His providential eyes,

from the numbering of the days of our life

to the numbering of the hairs on our head.

When we look at the world from that perspective,

it produces within us a response of reverence.

KEN GIRE

A mother is someone who dreams great dreams for you,

but then she lets you chase the dreams you have

for yourself and loves you just the same. In the end,

she believes in your dreams as much as you do.

God can do anything, you know—far more than you could

ever imagine or guess or request in your wildest dreams!

He does it not by pushing us around but by working within us,

his Spirit deeply and gently within us.

EPHESIANS 3:20–21 MSG

Children have neither past nor future;

they enjoy the present, which very few of us do.

JEAN DE LA BRUYÉRE

I'm going home." There may be sweeter phrases
in the English language—"I love you," for example.
But few phrases pack as much emotional wallop
as the simple expression of returning to the place
of one's birth, or to the haven of a house well lived in.
GARY BAUER

Mom, as often as I come back to your door,
your love meets me on the threshold,
and your serenity gives me comfort and peace.

Where we love is home,
Home that our feet may leave,
But not our hearts.
OLIVER WENDELL HOLMES

The Lord...blesses the home of the upright.
PROVERBS 3:33 NLT

Strength, rest, guidance, grace, help, sympathy, love—

all from God to us! What a list of blessings!

EVELYN STENBOCK

The Lord is great, and greatly to be praised....

The LORD made the heavens. Honour and majesty are before him:

strength and beauty are in his sanctuary....

Give unto the LORD glory and strength.

PSALM 96:4–7 KJV

You have no strength but what God gives

and you can have all the strength that God can give.

ANDREW MURRAY

God's love is like a river springing up in the Divine Substance

and flowing endlessly through His creation, filling all things

with life and goodness and strength.

THOMAS MERTON

The Lord is my strength and my shield;

my heart trusts in him, and I am helped.

My heart leaps for joy

and I will give thanks to him in song.

PSALM 28:7 NIV

God never abandons anyone on whom He has set His love;

nor does Christ, the good shepherd, ever lose track of His

sheep.... We need to "wait upon the Lord" in meditations

on His majesty, till we find our strength renewed through

the writing of these things upon our hearts.

J. I. PACKER

Should we feel at times disheartened and discouraged,

a simple movement of heart toward God will renew our

powers. Whatever He may demand of us, He will give us at

the moment the strength and courage that we need.

FRANÇOIS FÉNELON

To have someone who wants to absorb us, who wants
to understand the shape and structure of our lives, who will listen
for more than our words, is one of friendship's greatest gifts.

PAUL D. ROBBINS

A friend is always loyal, and a brother is born
to help in time of need.

PROVERBS 17:17 NLT

Many women...have buoyed me up in times of weariness
and stress. Each friend was important.... Their words have
seasoned my life. Influence, just like salt shaken out,
is hard to see, but its flavor is hard to miss.

PAM FARREL

Friendship is the fruit gathered from the trees planted in the rich
soil of love, and nurtured with tender care and understanding.

ALMA L. WEIXELBAUM

I am still determined to be cheerful and happy, in whatever situation I may be; for I have also learned from experience that the greater part of our happiness or misery depends upon our dispositions, and not upon our circumstances.

MARTHA WASHINGTON

Those who exalt themselves will be humbled, and those who humble themselves will be exalted.

MATTHEW 23:12 NIV

When we put people before possessions in our hearts, we are sowing seeds of enduring satisfaction.

BEVERLY LAHAYE

My heart is content with just knowing
Fulfillment that true friendship brings;
It fills to the brim, overflowing
With pleasure in life's "little things."

JUNE MASTERS BACHER

We can go through all the activities of our days

in joyful awareness of God's presence with whispered prayers

of praise and adoration flowing continuously from our hearts.

RICHARD J. FOSTER

It is right and good that we, for all things, at all times,

and in all places, give thanks and praise to You, O God.

We worship You, we confess to You, we praise You,

we bless You, we sing to You, and we give thanks to You: Maker,

Nourisher, Guardian, Healer, Lord, and Father of all.

LANCELOT ANDREWES

True worshipers will worship the Father in spirit and truth,

for the Father is seeking such people to worship him.

JOHN 4:23 ESV

Walk and talk and work and laugh with your friends, but behind

the scenes, keep up the life of simple prayer and inward worship.

THOMAS R. KELLY

Living the truth in your heart without compromise

brings kindness into the world.

EIGHTEENTH-CENTURY MONK

To follow truth as blind men long for light,

To do my best from dawn of day till night,

To keep my heart fit for His holy sight,

And answer when He calls.

This is my task.

MAUDE LOUISE RAY

I am amazed by the sayings of Christ.

They seem truer than anything I have ever read.

And they certainly turn the world upside down.

KATHERINE BUTLER HATHAWAY

There is no greater pleasure than bringing to the uncluttered, supple mind of a child the delight of knowing God and the many rich things He has given us to enjoy.

GLADYS M. HUNT

It's not what you think that influences your child; it's what you communicate.

CHARLES STANLEY

The time needed to talk to a child, time given to an impulse—only you can measure the value. For whatever ways you spend your time, it ought to pay high dividends in meeting physical needs and enriching the mind and spirit of each family member.

ALICE FULTON SKELSEY

Slow down and enjoy life. It's not only the scenery
you miss by going too fast—you also miss the sense
of where you are going and why.

EDDIE CANTOR

Half the joy of life is in little things taken on the run.
Let us run if we must—even the sands do that—but let us
keep our hearts young and our eyes open that nothing
worth our while shall escape us. And everything is worth
its while if we only grasp it and its significance.

VICTOR CHERBULIEZ

Dear friend, I pray that you may enjoy good health
and that all may go well with you,
even as your soul is getting along well.

3 JOHN 1:2 NIV

Where does the time go, Lord? I can't seem to get everything done in one day. Maybe I am trying to do too many things. No matter how busy it gets, help me to spend time with You every single day. If I don't, slow me down so I can. Thank You, Lord.

MARILYN JANSEN

When you have laboriously accomplished your daily task, go to sleep in peace. God is awake.

VICTOR HUGO

God has made everything beautiful for its own time. He has planted eternity in the human heart.

ECCLESIASTES 3:11 NLT

I believe that God is in me as the sun is in the color

and fragrance of a flower—the Light in my darkness,

the Voice in my silence.

HELEN KELLER

God has not promised skies always blue,

flower-strewn pathways all our lives through;

God has not promised sun without rain,

joy without sorrow, peace without pain.

But God has promised strength for the day,

rest for the labor, light for the way,

grace for the trials, help from above,

unfailing sympathy, undying love.

ANNIE JOHNSON FLINT

Your word is a lamp to my feet and a light for my path.

PSALM 119:105 NIV

Whether we are poets or parents or teachers or artists
or gardeners, we must start where we are and use what we have.
In the process of creation and relationship, what seems mundane
and trivial may show itself to be holy, precious, part of a pattern.

LUCI SHAW

To discipline a child produces wisdom....
Discipline your children, and they will give you
peace of mind and will make your heart glad.

PROVERBS 29:15, 17 NLT

The most important thing she'd learned over the years
was that there was no way to be a perfect mother
and a million ways to be a good one.

JILL CHURCHILL

God, help me to be honest

so my children will learn honesty.

Help me to be kind

so my children will learn kindness.

Help me to be faithful

so my children will learn faith.

Help me to love

so that my children will be loving.

MARIAN WRIGHT EDELMAN

Train up a child in the way he should go,

and when he is old he will not depart from it.

PROVERBS 22:6 NKJV

Kindness is the only service that will stand the storms of life and not wash out. It will wear well and be remembered long after the prism of politeness or the complexion of courtesy has faded away.

Notice words of compassion. Seek out deeds of kindness. These are like the doves from heaven, pointing out to you who are the ones blessed with inner grace and beauty.

CHRISTOPHER DE VINCK

The greatest thing a person can do for their heavenly Father is to be kind to some of His other children.... How easily it is done. How instantaneously it acts. How infallibly it is remembered.

HENRY DRUMMOND

Don't ever let yourself get so busy that you miss those little but important extras in life—the beauty of a day... the smile of a friend...the serenity of a quiet moment alone. For it is often life's smallest pleasures and gentlest joys that make the biggest and most lasting difference.

It doesn't take monumental feats to make the world a better place. It can be as simple as letting someone go ahead of you in a grocery line.

BARBARA JOHNSON

Let us consider how we may spur one another on toward love and good deeds.

HEBREWS 10:24 NIV

Though motherhood is the most important of all the professions—requiring more knowledge than any other department in human affairs—there was no attention given to preparation for this office.

ELIZABETH CADY STANTON

As a mother, my job is to take care of what is possible and trust God with the impossible.

RUTH BELL GRAHAM

Part of the curse of motherhood is never knowing if you're doing a good job. But part of the joy is realizing no one's really keeping score.

DALE HANSON BOURKE

Incredible as it may seem, God wants our companionship.
He wants to have us close to Him. He wants to be a father
to us, to shield us, to protect us, to counsel us,
and to guide us in our way through life.

BILLY GRAHAM

God still draws near to us in the ordinary,
commonplace, everyday experiences and places....
He comes in surprising ways.

HENRY GARIEPY

It is when things go wrong,
when good things do not happen,
when our prayers seem to have been lost,
that God is most present.

MADELEINE L'ENGLE

God has a wonderful plan for each person He has chosen.

He knew even before He created this world

what beauty He would bring forth from our lives.

LOUISE B. WYLY

Everyone has a unique role to fill in the world

and is important in some respect.

Everyone, including and perhaps especially you, is indispensable.

NATHANIEL HAWTHORNE

God gives us all gifts, special abilities that we are entrusted

with developing to help serve Him and serve others.

God has given each of you a gift from his great variety

of spiritual gifts. Use them well to serve one another.

1 PETER 4:10 NLT

Love in the heart wasn't put there to stay;

love isn't love 'til you give it away.

OSCAR HAMMERSTEIN II

If your gift is to encourage others, be encouraging.

If it is giving, give generously....

Don't just pretend to love other. Really love them.

ROMANS 12:8–9 NLT

Don't just get older, get better.

Live realistically. Give generously.

Adapt willingly. Trust fearlessly. Rejoice daily.

CHARLES SWINDOLL

Love is not the saying of the words

but the giving of the self.

ROBERT LANDER

Make my joy complete by being like-minded,

having the same love,

being one in spirit and of one mind.

PHILIPPIANS 2:2 NIV

Listening...means taking a vigorous,

human interest in what is being told us.

You can listen like a blank wall

or like a splendid auditorium

where every sound comes back fuller and richer.

ALICE DUER MILLER

Consider the lilies, how they grow: they neither toil

nor spin; and yet I say to you, even Solomon in all his glory

was not arrayed like one of these. If then God so clothes

the grass, which today is in the field and tomorrow

is thrown into the oven, how much more will He clothe you?

LUKE 12:27–28 NKJV

Something deep in all of us yearns for God's beauty,

and we can find it no matter where we are.

SUE MONK KIDD

Beauty puts a face on God. When we gaze at nature,

at a loved one, at a work of art, our soul immediately

recognizes and is drawn to the face of God.

MARGARET BROWNLEY

Those who know God as their Father know the whole secret.

They are His heirs, and may enter now into possession

of all that is necessary for their present needs.

HANNAH WHITALL SMITH

You care for the land and water it;

you enrich it abundantly.

The streams of God are filled with water

to provide the people with grain,

for so you have ordained it.

PSALM 65:9 NIV

God's gifts make us truly wealthy.

His loving supply never shall leave us wanting.

BECKY LAIRD

There was a place in childhood that I remember well,

And there a voice of sweetest tone bright fairy tales did tell.

SAMUEL LOVER

O Lord, you alone are my hope

I've trusted you, O LORD, from childhood.

Yes, you have been with me from birth;

from my mother's womb you have cared for me.

No wonder I am always praising you!

PSALM 71:5–6 NLT

The Creator thinks enough of you to have sent Someone
very special so that you might have life—
abundantly, joyfully, completely, and victoriously.

When we love someone, we want to be with them,
and we view their love for us with great honor even
if they are not a person of great status. For this reason—
and not because of our great status—God values our love.
So much, in fact, that He suffered greatly on our behalf.

JOHN CHRYSOSTOM

God shows his love for us in that while
we were still sinners, Christ died for us.

ROMANS 5:8 ESV

For the wisdom of the wisest being God has made
ends in wonder; and there is nothing on earth
so wonderful as the budding soul of a little child.

LUCY LARCOM

What a wildly wonderful world, GOD!
You made it all, with Wisdom at your side,
made earth overflow with your wonderful creations.

PSALM 104:24 MSG

All things bright and beautiful,
All creatures great and small,
All things wise and wonderful,
The Lord God made them all.

CECIL FRANCES ALEXANDER

I am convinced beyond a shadow of any doubt that the most
valuable pursuit we can embark upon is to know God.

KAY ARTHUR

Sometimes the laughter in mothering is the recognition of the ironies and absurdities. Sometimes, though, it's just pure, unthinking delight.

BARBARA SCHAPIRO

If children are to keep their inborn sense of wonder... they need the companionship of at least one adult who can share it, rediscovering with them the joy, excitement, and mystery of the world we live in.

RACHEL CARSON

My heart rejoices in the LORD! The LORD has made me strong.

1 SAMUEL 2:1 NLT

Joy is the feeling of grinning on the inside.

MELBA COLGROVE

Open wide the windows of our spirits and fill us full of light;
open wide the door of our hearts that we may receive
and entertain You with all the powers of our adoration.

CHRISTINA ROSSETTI

I find joy in receiving my children in prayer as gifts
from God. As I do it almost daily, I find that it enhances
my appreciation of them and my relationship with them.

JACK TAYLOR

Whate'er the care which breaks thy rest,
Whate'er the wish that swells thy breast;
Spread before God that wish, that care,
And change anxiety to prayer.

Rejoice always, pray without ceasing, give thanks
in all circumstances; for this is the will
of God in Christ Jesus for you.

1 THESSALONIANS 5:16–18 ESV

Unless you accept God's kingdom in the simplicity of a child, you'll never get in." Then, gathering the children up in his arms, [Jesus] laid his hands of blessing on them.

MARK 10:15–16 MSG

When you pray, do not try to express yourself in fancy words, for often it is the simple repetitious phrases of a little child that our Father in heaven finds most irresistible.

JOHN CLIMACUS

The wonder of our Lord is that He is so accessible to us in the common things of our lives: the cup of water... breaking of the bread...welcoming children into our arms... fellowship over a meal...giving thanks.

NANCIE CARMICHAEL

If you can help anybody even a little, be glad;

up the steps of usefulness and kindness,

God will lead you on to happiness and friendship.

MALTBIE D. BABCOCK

The older you get the more you realize

that kindness is synonymous with happiness.

LIONEL BARRYMORE

Be kind to one another, tenderhearted,

forgiving one another,

even as God in Christ forgave you.

EPHESIANS 4:32 NKJV

Recognizing the good in children
is one of the greatest gifts we can give to them.

We will not hide these truths from our children;
we will tell the next generation
about the glorious deeds of the LORD,
about his power and his mighty wonders.

PSALM 78:4 NLT

What parent can tell when some fragmentary gift
of knowledge or wisdom will enrich her children's lives?

HELENA RUBINSTEIN

Simplicity will enable you to leap lightly.
Increasingly you will find yourself living in a state of grace,
finding...the sacred in the ordinary,
the mystical in the mundane.

DAVID YOUNT

A devout life does bring wealth, but it's the rich simplicity
of being yourself before God. Since we entered the world
penniless and will leave it penniless, if we have bread
on the table and shoes on our feet, that's enough.

1 TIMOTHY 6:6–8 MSG

It isn't the great big pleasures that count the most;
it's making a great deal out of the little ones.

JEAN WEBSTER

Motherhood is...the biggest on-the-job
training program in existence today.
ERMA BOMBECK

More so than any other human relationship,
in fact, overwhelmingly more, motherhood means
being instantly interruptible, responsive, and responsible.

Cast your cares on the LORD and he will sustain you.
PSALM 55:22 NIV

Mother had a thousand thoughts to get through within a day,
and...most of these were about avoiding disaster.
NATALIE KUSZ

Giving is the secret of a healthy life…
not necessarily money, but whatever one has
of encouragement and sympathy and understanding.
JOHN D. ROCKEFELLER JR.

Be happy with what you have and are,
be generous with both,
and you won't have to hunt for happiness.
WILLIAM E. GLADSTONE

Love is not getting, but giving….
It is goodness and honor and peace and pure living—
yes, love is that and it is the best thing in the world
and the thing that lives the longest.
HENRY VAN DYKE

Having someone who understands is a great blessing
for ourselves. Being someone who understands
is a great blessing to others.

JANETTE OKE

Oh, the comfort, the inexpressible comfort of feeling safe
with a person—having neither to weigh thoughts nor measure
words, but pouring them all right out just as they are,
chaff and grain together, certain that a faithful hand
will take and sift them, keep what is worth keeping and then,
with the breath of kindness, blow the rest away.

DINAH MARIA MULOCK CRAIK

We should all have one person who knows
how to bless us despite the evidence.

PHYLLIS THEROUX

Every time you smile at someone, it is an action of love,

a gift to that person, a beautiful thing.

MOTHER TERESA

The Lord is my chosen portion and my cup...

indeed, I have a beautiful inheritance.

PSALM 16:5–6 ESV

Isn't it a wonderful morning? The world looks like

something God had just imagined for His own pleasure.

LUCY MAUD MONTGOMERY

You are God's created beauty

and the focus of His affection and delight.

JANET L. SMITH

I must simply be thankful, and I am, for all the Lord has provided

for me, whether big or small in the eyes of someone else.

MABEL P. ADAMSON

You can trust God right now to supply all

your needs for today. And if your needs

are more tomorrow, His supply will be greater also.

Throughout the Bible, when God asked someone to do something,

methods, means, materials, and specific directions were always

provided. That person had one thing to do: obey.

ELISABETH ELLIOT

Take the gift of this moment and make something

beautiful of it. Few worthwhile experiences just happen,

memories are made on purpose.

GLORIA GAITHER

Gratitude is the memory of the heart.

LYDIA MARIA CHILD

How dear to the heart are the scenes of my childhood,

when fond recollection presents them to view.

SAMUEL WOODWORTH

Memory is the treasury and guardian of all things.

CICERO

The Lord's chief desire is to reveal Himself to you and,
in order for Him to do that, He gives you abundant grace.
The Lord gives you the experience of enjoying His presence.
He touches you, and His touch is so delightful that,
more than ever, you are drawn inwardly to Him.

MADAME JEANNE GUYON

You're all I want in heaven! You're all I want on earth....
I'm in the very presence of GOD—
oh, how refreshing it is! I've made Lord GOD my home.
GOD, I'm telling the world what you do!

PSALM 73:25, 28 MSG

Life need not be easy to be joyful.
Joy is not the absence of trouble, but the presence of Christ.

WILLIAM VANDERHOVEN

Ask any four-year-old boy, "Who's the most beautiful woman in the world?" His mommy! Ask any grown daughter caring for her aging mother the same question, and you'll get the same answer.... Moms spend a lifetime humbling themselves in taking care of others. Nothing is more attractive.

Therefore, as God's chosen people, holy and dearly loved, clothe yourselves with compassion, kindness, humility, gentleness and patience.

COLOSSIANS 3:12 NIV

As God's workmanship, we deserve to be treated, and to treat ourselves, with affection and affirmation, regardless of our appearance or performance.

MARY ANN MAYO

Not everyone possesses boundless energy

or a conspicuous talent. We are not equally blessed

with great intellect or physical beauty or emotional strength.

But we have all been given the same ability to be faithful.

GIGI GRAHAM TCHIVIDJIAN

No one can arrive from being talented alone.

God gives talent, work transforms talent into genius.

ANNA PAVLOVA

Whatever you do, whether in word or deed, do it all in the name

of the Lord Jesus, giving thanks to God the Father through him.

COLOSSIANS 3:17 NIV

Do all the good you can

By all the means you can

In all the ways you can

In all the places you can

To all the people you can

As long as ever you can.

JOHN WESLEY

A mother can see beauty

In the very smallest thing

For there's a little bit of heaven

In a small child's offering.

KATHERINE NELSON DAVIS

My childhood home was the home of a woman

with a genius for inventing daily life,

who found happiness in the simplest of gestures.

LAURA FRONTY

With our children who thrive on simple pleasures,

our work and our entire society can be renewed.

SARA WENGER SHENK

It is always wise to stop wishing for things

long enough to enjoy

the fragrance of those now flowering.

PATRICE GIFFORD

In all ranks of life the human heart yearns for the beautiful,

and the beautiful things that God makes are His gift to all alike.

HARRIET BEECHER STOWE

Loving Creator, help me reawaken my childlike sense

of wonder at the delights of Your world!

MARILYN MORGAN HELLEBERG

Women of adventure have conquered their fates and know

how to live exciting and fulfilling lives right where they are.

They have learned to reinvent themselves and find creative

ways to enjoy the world and their place in it.

They know how to take mini-vacations, stop and smell

the roses, and live fully in the moment.

BARBARA JENKINS

Let the day suffice, with all its joys and failings,

its little triumphs and defeats.... Happily, if sleepily,

welcome evening as a time of rest,

and let it slip away, losing nothing.

KATHLEEN NORRIS

I have learned the secret of being content

in any and every situation, whether well fed or hungry,

whether living in plenty or in want.

PHILIPPIANS 4:12 NIV

Love never gives up.

Love cares more for others than for self.

Love doesn't want what it doesn't have.

Love doesn't strut...

Isn't always "me first,"

Doesn't fly off the handle,

Doesn't keep score of the sins of others...

Takes pleasure in the flowering of truth,

Puts up with anything,

Trusts God always,

Always looks for the best,

Never looks back,

But keeps going to the end.

1 CORINTHIANS 13:4–7 MSG

Love. No greater theme can be emphasized.

No stronger message can be proclaimed.

No finer song can be sung. No better truth can be imagined.

CHARLES SWINDOLL

See each morning a world made anew,

as if it were the morning of the very first day...

treasure and use it, as if it were

the final hour of the very last day.

FAY HARTZELL ARNOLD

Store up for yourselves treasures in heaven,

where moth and rust do not destroy,

and where thieves do not break in and steal.

For where your treasure is,

there your heart will be also.

MATTHEW 6:20–21 NIV

Every material goal, even if it is met, will pass away.

But the heritage of children is timeless.

Our children are our messages to the future.

BILLY GRAHAM

I will sing of the mercies of the LORD forever;

with my mouth will I make known

Your faithfulness to all generations.

PSALM 89:1 NKJV

There is nothing quite so deeply satisfying as the solidarity

of a family united across the generations

and miles by a common faith and history.

SARA WENGER SHENK

Life is no brief candle to me. It is a...splendid torch...

and I want to make it burn as brightly as possible

before handing it over to future generations.

GEORGE BERNARD SHAW

Can you measure the worth of a sunbeam,

The worth of a treasured smile,

The value of love and of giving,

The things that make life worthwhile?...

Can you measure the value of friendship,

Of knowing that someone is there,

Of faith and of hope and of courage,

A treasured and goodly share?

GARNETT ANN SCHULTZ

We must not, in trying to think about how we can

make a big difference, ignore the small daily differences

we can make which, over time, add up to big

differences that we often cannot foresee.

MARIAN WRIGHT EDELMAN

Let your light shine before others so that they may see your

good works and give glory to your Father who is in heaven.

MATTHEW 5:16 ESV

What we feel, think, and do this moment influences both our
present and the future in ways we may never know. Begin.
Start right where you are. Consider your possibilities and find
inspiration...to add more meaning and zest to your life.

ALEXANDRA STODDARD

The blossom cannot tell what becomes of its fragrance as it drifts
away, just as no person can tell what becomes of her influence
as she continues through life. The fullness of our heart is expressed
in our eyes, in our touch, in what we write, in what we say,
in the way we walk, the way we receive, the way we need.

MOTHER TERESA

God will never walk away from his people,
never desert his precious people.
Rest assured that justice is on its way
and every good heart put right.

PSALM 94:14–15 MSG

We give thanks for the darkness of the night where lies the world of dreams.... Give us good dreams and memory of them so that we may carry their poetry and mystery into our daily lives.... Let us restore the night and reclaim it as a sanctuary of peace, where silence shall be music to our hearts and darkness shall throw light upon our souls.

MICHAEL LEUNIG

Grace and peace to you from God our Father and from the Lord Jesus Christ.

ROMANS 1:7 NIV

Only God gives true peace—a quiet gift He sets within us just when we think we've exhausted our search for it.

O heavenly Father, protect and bless all things that have breath: guard them from all evil and let them sleep in peace.

ALBERT SCHWEITZER

I wish I had a box,

the biggest I could find,

I'd fill it right up to the brim

with everything that's kind.

A box without a lock, of course,

and never any key;

for everything inside that box

would then be offered free.

Grateful words for joys received

I'd freely give away.

Oh, let us open wide a box

of praise for every day.

Each day is a treasure box of gifts from God,

just waiting to be opened. Open your gifts with excitement.

You will find forgiveness attached to ribbons of joy.

You will find love wrapped in sparkling gems.

JOAN CLAYTON

May the LORD richly bless both you

and your children.

PSALM 115:14 NLT

Whenever I need help being a mother,

I remember my mother and grandmother,

women who planted seeds of wisdom in my soul,

like a secret garden, to flower even in the bitterest cold.

JUDITH TOWSE-ROBERTS

Heavenly Father, please give me wisdom in daily protecting

my children. Whether it's concerning the people they come

in contact with, the television and videos they watch,

or the many other issues that affect them, may I be aware

of my responsibility to guide and nurture their minds. Amen.

KIM BOYCE

Teach us to number our days aright,

that we may gain a heart of wisdom.

PSALM 90:12 NIV

Jesus said, "Let the little children come to me, and do not hinder them, for the kingdom of heaven belongs to such as these."

MATTHEW 19:14 NIV

The most successful parents are those who have the skill to get behind the eyes of a child, seeing what they see, thinking what they think, feeling what they feel.

DR. JAMES DOBSON

It is a special gift to be able to view the world through the eyes of a child.

Ellie Claire® Gift & Paper Expressions
Franklin, TN 37067
EllieClaire.com
Ellie Claire is a registered trademark of Worthy Media, Inc.

Her Children Call Her Blessed Journal
© 2017 by Ellie Claire
Published by Ellie Claire, an imprint of Worthy Publishing Group, a division of
Worthy Media, Inc.

ISBN 978-1-63326-187-7

Stock or custom editions of Ellie Claire titles may be purchased in bulk
for educational, business, ministry, fundraising, or sales promotional use.
For information, please e-mail info@EllieClaire.com

Art from Creative Market | creativemarket.com
Cover and interior design by Sally Haukas
Typesetting by Jeff Jansen | AestheticSoup.net

Printed in China

1 2 3 4 5 6 7 8 9 RRD 21 20 19 18 17